The Basic Elements of Sports Series

ZUMBROTA PUBLIC LIBRARY
100 WEST AVENUE
ZUMBROTA, MN 55992

GOLF'S TIMELESS FUNDAMENTAL

**Written by Jeffrey J. Peshut
Illustrated by Jay Moore**

D1712811

ICS BOOKS, Inc.
Merrillville, IN

GOLF'S TIMELESS FUNDAMENTAL

Copyright © 1997 by Jeffrey J. Peshut
10 9 8 7 6 5 4 3 2 1

All rights reserved, including the right to reproduce this book or portions thereof in any form or by any means, electronic or mechanical, including photocopying, recording, unless authorization is obtained, in writing, from the publisher. All inquiries should be addressed to ICS Books, Inc, 1370 E. 86th Place, Merrillville, IN 46410

Printed in the U.S.A.

Published by:
ICS BOOKS, Inc
1370 E. 86th Place
Merrillville, IN 46410
800-541-7323

Library of Congress Cataloging-in-Publication Data

Peshut, Jeffrey J.
   Golf's timeless fundamental / by Jeffrey J. Peshut.
   p.   cm.
   Originally published: Provo, Utah : Thanks American Press, 1991
   ISBN 1-57034-065-X (pb)
   1. Birds--Wit and humor. 2. American wit and humor. I. Title.
PN6231.B46G66   1997
818' .5407--dc21
                                                 96-51623
                                                      CIP

DEDICATION

To Cydney

ACKNOWLEDGEMENTS

Many people contributed to turning the idea for this book into reality. My special thanks to Tom Todd of ICS Books for taking a chance with a first-time author. My special thanks also to Jay Moore for his masterful illustrations and Terry Rigg and Tedd Aurelius of ARTComm for their contributions to the design and layout of this book.

Thanks to my good friends Chris Rule, Jeff Castleton, Mike Duffy, Scott Paramski, Steve Murchison and Bill Haring for their encouragement and support throughout the two years it took to complete this project. Thanks also to my golf instructor, Mike McGetrick, who is helping me to better learn the "other" fundamentals.

Finally, thanks to all of the writers whose works have contributed to the great body of work surrounding the golf swing. Many of their ideas laid the foundation for the idea behind this book.

TABLE OF CONTENTS

INTRODUCTION

Are you frustrated with your golf game? Do you want to get better but see little improvement in your game, no matter how much you practice, how many lessons you take or how many instruction books or magazine articles that you read? Can you characterize your progress in golf as "one step forward, two steps back"?

Do you often hit the ball well on the driving range, but then "lose it" on the course? When you are hitting your driver well, do you find yourself missing your irons? When you are nailing your irons, does your putting stroke disappear? Do you play like a pro on one hole, and like a duffer on the next? Do you ever wonder why you just can't seem to pull it together all at one time? And then keep it together?

Does it seem to you that the really good players know something that you don't know? Have you ever thought that modern golf instruction is leaving out something important?

THIS BOOK WAS WRITTEN FOR YOU

If you answered yes to any of these questions, then this book was written for you!

In this book, you will learn the timeless fundamental that all good players and teachers know, but few if any can explain. Not only will you learn this timeless fundamental, but even more importantly you will learn how to incorporate it into your golf swing to hit the golf ball longer, straighter and more consistently than you ever have before. You will also learn to incorporate the fundamental into your short game to help you improve your touch, score lower and win more.

In a very short time, you will experience an increase in your self-confidence on the golf course and gain greater admiration and respect from the members of your foursome.

WHY I WROTE THIS BOOK

Most golf instruction books available today have been written by famous players and instructors. These books typically focus on key fundamentals such as grip, stance, posture, aim, and ball position. They also illustrate key body positions that the golf swing passes through and attempt to explain key swing movements. These body positions may include the address, back swing, top of the back swing, transition, down swing, impact, follow-through and finish.

Many provide an overview of the short game, including pitching, chipping, putting and sand play. Some even include a discussion of practice techniques and drills, course management skills and the "mental" side of the game.

Few, if any, adequately convey the true essence of the golf swing.

That's not to say that these books aren't very valuable and useful. Many are excellent with respect to the subjects they address. In fact, I've mentioned some of my favorites in Chapter 4.

It's just that they are incomplete. They fail to give you the last few pieces to the puzzle that you need to see the whole picture. In some cases they go to the other extreme and give you extra pieces that — while intellectually interesting — are really unnecessary to complete the picture. Often these extra pieces reflect the authors' personal styles rather than true swing fundamentals.

Of course, on some level — whether consciously or unconsciously — these authors must understand the fundamental introduced in this book. Most have learned it at a very young age through a combination of athletic talent, expert instruction, unrelenting determination, and virtually unlimited opportunities to practice and play.

By hitting hundreds and thousands of golf balls each day, they learned to "feel" the presence of golf's timeless fundamental in their swings. It's almost as if they learned through osmosis. The very methods by which they learned this fundamental, however, leaves them at a loss for words to explain it to others.

That hasn't kept them from trying. The more scientific or "left brained" among them have tried to explain this fundamental in terms of "mechanics". The more artistic or "right brained" among them have tried to explain it in terms of "feel". Based upon the large numbers of golfers not playing up to their potential, neither group has been as effective as I am sure they would like to be.

That's why I wrote this book. It is intended to help you to learn golf's timeless fundamental without having to hit hundreds and thousands of golf balls each day. While there will be some discussion of mechanics and feel, it doesn't rely heavily on either one. Instead, it takes a third approach — a combination of both science and art — from which you will develop correct mechanics and the correct feel. This third approach is simple and easy to learn.

At this point I want to be careful not to mislead you. Learning to play golf up to your potential will still require considerable time, attention and effort from you. Like other areas of your life, there is no substitute for clear goals, hard work, and the determination to succeed. There is certainly no substitute for regular practice and regular play.

After you read this book, however, you will be spending your practice time in a much more effective manner. You will be practicing and playing with the entire picture in mind, not just a part of it. The result will be steady and consistent progress towards your goal — whatever it may be — instead of the "one step forward, two steps back" experience referred to earlier.

WHAT YOU WILL FIND IN THIS BOOK

This book is divided into 6 chapters. Let me take a minute to preview them with you.

Chapter 1 reveals golf's timeless fundamental to you in a straight-forward, easy-to-understand approach. Not only will you learn what to do, you will learn why it works. To help you understand the fundamental, Chapter 1 also defines several terms and concepts that are routinely mis-used by both amateurs and professionals alike.

In Chapter 2, you get step-by-step instructions on how to find your golf swing tempo, and once you find it, how to keep it on every swing. In Chapter 3, you will learn how to master the golf swing rhythm, which is essential to learning golf's timeless fundamental.

Chapter 4 brings it all together to teach you how to incorporate golf's timeless fundamental into the full golf swing. Chapter 4 also explains how the golf swing's other fundamentals — including grip, stance, aim, posture and ball position — relate to the fundamental introduced in this book.

In Chapter 5, you will learn how to consistently apply golf's timeless fundamental on every swing, whether a full swing or a partial swing.

The book concludes with a "playing lesson" in Chapter 6. It begins with your arrival at the golf course before the lesson, and concludes with several holes of golf.

ABOUT THE AUTHOR

Before turning to Chapter 1, let me tell you a little about myself. I am not a professional golfer or even a teaching professional for that matter. I have spent part of my career practicing law, and am currently working for a national real estate advisory and investment management firm.

Because of time constraints, I usually play golf on one day over the weekend. If I am lucky, I'll get to play during the week every now and then, and occasionally hit a bucket of balls in the evening after work. I think of myself as an average golfer, who — through a fair amount of study and experimentation — discovered a golf fundamental that for the most part has gone previously unexplained.

For years I struggled to take my game to the next level. I took lessons. I read books and magazine articles. I watched videos. I spent hour after hour on the practice range. I tried everything I could think of! But still, I wasn't seeing the results I was looking for. I knew that something was missing.

Then I discovered the fundamental revealed to you in this book. I saw an immediate and dramatic improvement in both my ball striking and my short game. Everything I had ever learned about golf suddenly came together. I found a new sense of hope and optimism about my potential to play golf at a higher level than I ever had before.

Probably the biggest change came in the area of consistency. Like you, I typically hit many excellent shots during a round of golf. For every good shot, however, I hit many more disappointing shots than I'd care to admit. The fundamental introduced in this book will allow you to hit a lot more good shots and a lot fewer bad shots. Not only that, but it will improve the quality of your bad shots.

When you come right down to it, isn't that our goal? To hit more good shots and fewer bad shots? And to improve the quality of our bad shots? After all, it has been said by many that you measure the quality of a golfer not by the quality of their best shots, but by the quality of their worst shots.

This book is my attempt to share my discovery with you. Although this book will help golfers at every level, it is primarily aimed at the average golfer who wants to get better. I guess you might say that it is a book written by an average golfer for average golfers. I know that if it can work for me, it can also work for you!

A LABOR OF LOVE

I developed my love for the game of golf in my teens, while caddying at Knollwood Club in Lake Forest, Illinois. My connection to the game of golf grew stronger when I received a scholarship to the University of Illinois from the Evans Scholars Foundation.

For those of you not familiar with it, the Evans Scholars program was founded in the early 1930's by Charles E. "Chick" Evans, Jr., who between 1910 and 1920 was one of the world's greatest golfers. In 1916 he won both the U.S. Amateur and the U.S. Open, a feat equaled only by the legendary Bobby Jones in his grand slam year of 1930. Today, the Evans Scholars program is the largest privately funded college scholarship program in the world.

In the fall of 1977, during my junior year at the University of Illinois, I had the honor of spending a day with Chick Evans in downtown Chicago while writing an article on him for the Daily Illini newspaper. We talked about caddying, we talked about golf and we talked about how proud he was of the Evans Scholars program and the many students it was helping to receive a college education. As I traveled by train back to Champaign-Urbana later that day, I was inspired by the impact the life of this one man had made on the lives of so many young people.

Chick Evans died in 1979 at the age of 89. Looking back, I realize that I have Chick to thank not only for providing me with a college education, but also for providing me with much of the inspiration I've needed to write this book. This year is the 80th anniversary of Chick's "double crown". As a way to honor his memory, and as a way to pass along part of the gift that Chick gave to me, ten percent of the royalties I receive from the sale of this book will be donated to the Evans Scholars Foundation.

AN OPEN INVITATION

Once you have had a chance to read this book and to begin incorporating golf's timeless fundamental into your golf swing, I invite you to contact me to let me know how you are doing. I have personally experienced the highs and lows associated with the learning process, and know what you will be going through as you begin to improve your golf swing.

I want to make myself available to you to congratulate you on your successes, and to help you to work through your frustrations. I want you to do well and am willing to do what I can to help you to make that happen. Feel free to write me in care of the publisher. They will pass your letters along to me.

Good luck with your new golf swing. I hope to hear from you soon!

Your friend in golf,

Littleton, Colorado
June, 1996

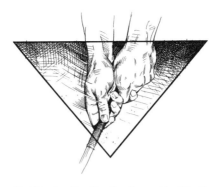

Discover Golf's Timeless Fundamental

Swing Your Hands Like A Pendulum!

If you examine the golf swings of all the great players throughout the history of the game, you will notice that they all have one thing in common. They all swing their hands like a pendulum during their golf swings. This is true regardless of the length of the club or the length of the swing. Whether a 300-yard drive or a 3-foot putt, their hands swing like a pendulum.

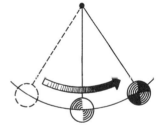

But don't just take my word for it; check for yourself. The next time you are watching a golf tournament on television, focus closely on how the pros move their hands. Ignore everything else. Focus only on their hands.

Notice the smooth, rhythmic swinging motion. Notice that the tempo is the same for every swing. Notice how their hands travel along the same arc on every swing. Notice how their hands travel the same distance on the back swing as on the follow-through. These are all characteristics of a pendulum.

It won't take you very long to notice that they all swing their hands like a pendulum with every club, and with every swing.

Once you see what I'm talking about, congratulate yourself. You just discovered golf's timeless fundamental! The rest of this book is devoted to teaching you how to incorporate this fundamental into your golf swing.

WHY SWING YOUR HANDS LIKE A PENDULUM?

Why do the great players swing their hands like a pendulum during their golf swings? Because they have learned that this is the best way to hit a golf ball.

By swinging their hands like a pendulum:

> -They create a tremendous amount of centrifugal force, which is the greatest force people can generate with their own bodies. You cannot move your hands any faster than you can swing them. The creation of centrifugal force translates into maximum club head speed, which in turn translates into maximum distance.

> -Their hands always swings on the same plane. If they align their body and the club properly, swinging on the same plane translates into pin-point accuracy.

> -Their hands travel on the same arc or path every time. This means the club head also travels on the same arc every time. A repeating arc guarantees consistency.

> -They are able to control the length of a shot with a particular club by simply controlling the length of the swing arc. Controlling the length of a shot, especially with the scoring clubs, is the key to improved touch and lower scores.

Distance, accuracy and consistency. Improved touch and lower scores. That 's why they swing their hands like a pendulum!

WHAT ABOUT SWINGING THE CLUB HEAD
LIKE A PENDULUM?

At this point, I'm sure some of you are saying to your-selves, "What the heck is this guy talking about? We don't hit the golf ball with our hands, we hit the golf ball with the club head!"

"What about swinging the club head like a pendulum?"

I believe that most of the problems in our golf swings are a direct result of our conscious efforts to manipulate the club head with our hands. Of course we hit the golf ball with the club head. Of course the club head swings like a pendulum to get to the golf ball. But this is the result of what we do with our bodies and our hands as we hold the golf club, not the cause of it.

If we hold the golf club properly, align ourselves and the golf club to the ball properly, and then swing our hands like a pendulum, centrifugal force and the law of conser-vation of angular momentum will take care of the club head. Swinging the club head requires no conscious effort from us.

It's just like hammering a nail. We take hold of the ham-mer, tap the nail a few times to get it started and to get our aim, and then swing our hand several times while holding the hammer. We aren't conscious of manipulat-ing the hammer head with our hand. The centrifugal force generated by our swinging hand takes care of it!

Another way to settle this question about swinging the club head like a pendulum is to approach it from the standpoint of cause and effect. It is easy to cause the club head to swing like a pendulum, without necessarily hav-ing the effect of swinging your hands like a pendulum. It is difficult, however, to cause your hands to swing like a pendulum, without also having the effect of swinging the club head like a pendulum.

So, take hold of a club, address the ball, relax and swing your hands like a pendulum during your golf swing!

HOW A PENDULUM SWINGS

Before you can learn how to swing your hands like a pendulum during your golf swing, you must first understand how a pendulum swings.

A Simple Pendulum

A simple pendulum consists of a weight, suspended by a string, from a fixed axis known as the suspension point. Several definite laws or principles govern how a simple pendulum swings.

If you hold the string of a simple pendulum between your thumb and index finger, and swing the weight back and forth at a speed that keeps the string taut, the string will swing freely along an arc. The swing, always in the same vertical plane, is produced because of the force of gravity.

The weight always travels the same distance on the upswing as it does on the downswing. The time it takes the weight to travel along its arc and back again to the starting point is called the period of the swing. The weight achieves its maximum speed at the bottom of its arc, located directly below the suspension point, which is

The **Period** of The
Simple Pendulum

Illustration 1-1

known as the equilibrium point. (See Illustration 1-1)
The period of a simple pendulum is divisible into four
equal beats or counts. The first beat is from the starting
point to the bottom of the arc. The second beat is from
the bottom of the arc to the farthest point of the swing.
The third beat is from that point back to the bottom of
the arc, and the fourth beat is from the bottom of the arc
back to the starting point. This division of the period
into four equal beats or counts is known as the rhythm of
the simple pendulum. (See Illustration 1-2)

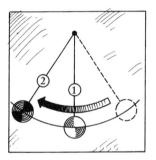 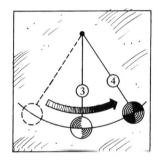

The **Rhythm** of The
Simple Pendulum

Illustration 1-2

The period of a simple pendulum depends solely upon the length of the string. It has nothing to do with the amount of weight at the end of the string or the length of the arc. In other words, for a string of a given length, the time it takes the weight to travel along its arc and back again to the starting point remains the same no matter how heavy the weight or how long its arc. This phenomenon is called isochronism. (See Illustration 1-3)

The **Isochronism** of
The Simple Pendulum

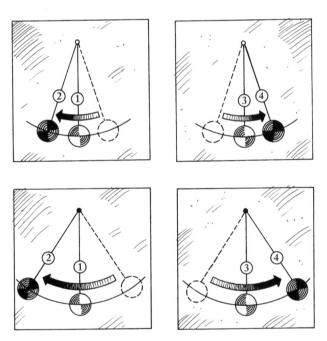

Illustration 1-3

Keep in mind that the speed of the weight at the equilibrium point must increase as the length of the arc increases, and must decrease as the length of the arc decreases. After all, the swinging weight is covering a longer or shorter distance but in the same amount of time.

THE GOLF SWING PENDULUM

The golf swing pendulum is governed by the same laws and principles as the simple pendulum, with only minor exceptions.

The golf swing pendulum consists of the hands and club as the weight, the two arms as the strings, and the top of the spine as the suspension point. (See Illustration 1-4.) The top of the spine is the suspension point because the turning shoulders provide the primary source of support and control for the swinging hands, and the shoulders rotate around a fixed axis located at the top of the spine. As you will learn, you swing your hands like a pendulum through the turning motion of your shoulders, especially your left shoulder.

The **Golf Swing** Pendulum

Illustration 1-4

Unlike the simple pendulum, which has only one string, the golf swing pendulum is slightly more complex and actually has two strings which effectively do the work of one string. Of the two strings, the left arm is the primary string because gravity and centrifugal force keep it relatively taut from address, to the top of the back swing, past impact, and well into the follow-through. By comparison, the right arm is relaxed at address and begins bending relatively early during the back swing. Centrifugal force does not pull it taut until well into the follow-through.

Even though the golf swing pendulum has two strings, it is the distance from the top of the spine to the hands — not the distance from the shoulders to the hands — that establishes the length of the string for the golf swing pendulum.

The angle of the plane is another way in which the golf swing pendulum differs from the simple pendulum. Recall that the simple pendulum swings on a vertical plane. The golf swing pendulum, on the other hand, swings on an inclined plane which runs from the top of the spine to the hands. This inclined plane is the result of the forward tilt of the spine at address.

Like the simple pendulum, the golf swing pendulum has a definite period and a definite rhythm. With the golf swing pendulum, however, we use the term tempo to describe the period of the swing. Understanding the period and rhythm of the golf swing pendulum, and the related concept of timing, is essential to learning how to swing your hands like a pendulum during your golf swing.

Tempo, Rhythm And Timing Defined

Tempo, rhythm and timing, are three terms that are routinely misused by both amateur and professional golfers alike. Most golfers use these terms interchangeably, when in fact they each have very distinct and separate meanings.

Webster's Dictionary defines tempo as, "the rate of speed of a musical piece or passage" or "rate of motion or activity: PACE." In music, the tempo or speed of the music refers to how quickly or slowly a musical piece or passage is to be played. It is measured by the number of beats per minute.

In golf, tempo refers to the time it takes for the hands to go from the start of the swing to the finish of the swing. It represents the overall speed of the swing. The concept of tempo in the golf swing is identical to the concept of the period in the simple pendulum. You will learn that like the tempo of a musical piece or passage, your golf swing tempo can also be measured in number of beats per minute.

Webster's defines rhythm as an "ordered recurrent alternation of strong and weak elements in the flow of sound and silence in speech" and "movement or fluctuation marked by the regular recurrence or natural flow of related elements." We have already discussed the concept of rhythm in connection with the simple pendulum. In music, rhythm refers to the accent on or emphasis of certain beats in a recurring pattern. For example, consider the difference between a waltz rhythm, and a march rhythm. Keep in mind that a particular rhythm can be played at an infinite variety of tempos or speeds.

In golf, rhythm refers to how the total time of the swing is apportioned among the various parts of the swing. As you will see, the rhythm of the golf swing pendulum is rooted in the rhythm of the simple pendulum.

"... the rhythm of the golf swing pendulum is rooted in the rhythm of the simple pendulum."

Finally, according to Webster's, timing is the "selection... for maximum effect of the precise moment for beginning or doing something." In golf, the "doing something" is hitting the golf ball with the club head. Thus, good timing is swinging your hands so that the club head hits the golf ball at the precise moment necessary to have the "maximum effect". This precise moment occurs when the swinging hands reach the bottom of their arc or their equilibrium point.

HOW TO SWING YOUR HANDS LIKE A PENDULUM

Now that you understand that your goal is to swing your hands like a pendulum, and that you have learned about the principles that govern how a pendulum swings, all that remains is for you to learn a reliable way to swing your hands like a pendulum during your golf swing. You have learned the "what" and "why", now you must learn the "how". The remainder of this book will provide you with a step-by-step method of doing just that. You will first learn how to find your golf swing tempo, then how to master the golf swing rhythm, next how to set up your golf swing pendulum and finally how to combine all of the steps to allow you to swing your hands like a pendulum.

SUMMARY

In this chapter, you discovered that swinging your hands like a pendulum during your golf swing is golf's timeless fundamental. It is the one thing all great players have in common.

You also took the first step towards learning how to swing your hands like a pendulum during your golf swing by learning the essential elements and characteristics of the golf swing pendulum. Two essential elements of the golf swing pendulum are tempo and rhythm.

In the next chapter, you will learn how to find your golf swing tempo, and once you have found it, how to keep it on every swing.

How To Find Your Golf Swing Tempo

In this chapter, you will learn how to find your golf swing tempo, which is the next step towards learning how to swing your hands like a pendulum during your golf swing.

Understanding Your Golf Swing Tempo

Your golf swing tempo is just that — your golf swing tempo. Your golf swing tempo is as personal to you as your fingerprints. Like the period of a simple pendulum, it depends solely upon the length of the string. Because the distance from the top of the spine to the hands is different for each person, the golf swing tempo must also be different for each person.

A swing that takes a relatively short period of time is said to have a fast tempo. A swing that takes a relatively long period of time is said to have a slow tempo. For example, consider the different tempos of Nick Price and Ernie Els.

Your golf swing tempo is, however, the same for every club. It is also the same for every swing with a particular club. Again, the principle of isochronism states that the period of the pendulum swing depends solely upon the length of the string, and has nothing to do with the length of the arc. Even though the length of the swing arc differs from club to club, and swing to swing, the length of the string is constant. The distance from the top of your spine to your hands hasn't changed!

Of course, your hands move faster at the equilibrium point with the longer clubs because your hands are traveling along a longer arc with the longer clubs. Your hands also move faster at the equilibrium point in a full swing with a particular club than they do in a partial swing with a particular club. Once again, your hands are traveling along a longer arc with the full swing than they are with the partial swing. Still, the time it takes your hands to go from the start of the swing to the finish of the swing is the same for every club and every swing.

One last point. You have only one optimum golf swing tempo that is the same for every club and every swing. You will play your best golf when you are swinging at your optimum golf swing tempo.

To help you to grasp this point, swing a simple pendulum with your thumb and index finger. As you swing it back and forth, you can increase or decrease the length of the swing arc, but you cannot affect the period or tempo of the swing. If you try to change the period or tempo, the weight will leave its arc and you will lose the swinging motion. This same concept holds true for the golf swing pendulum and explains inconsistencies in your game when you fail to swing at your optimum golf swing tempo.

A simple pendulum has only one optimum period or tempo. The same is true for the golf swing pendulum. Finding your optimum golf swing tempo is the next steps towards learning to swing your hands like a pendulum during your golf swing.

Preparing To Find Your Golf Swing Tempo

The following preliminary drill will help to prepare you to find your golf swing tempo:

STEP ONE: Stand erect, with the outsides of your feet as wide as the outsides of your shoulders, your hands hanging naturally at your sides, and your eyes looking straight ahead at the horizon. Make sure that there is no tension in either your shoulders or your arms.

STEP TWO: Curl your left hand into a fist, again making sure that there is no tension in your left shoulder, upper arm or forearm. If you squeeze your upper arm and forearm with your opposite hand, it should feel "soft" and relaxed, not "hard" and tense.

STEP THREE: Keeping your feet in place, begin swinging your left hand to the front and to the back at your side, similar to the way you swing your hands at your side when you are walking. Begin by swinging your hand in 2 to 3 foot arcs, and then gradually extend the length of the arc until your hand reaches shoulder height at the farthest point of its swing. Go ahead and let your shoulders turn to the right and to the left in response to the swinging motion of your hand.

STEP FOUR: As you swing your hand to the front and to the back, count to four in time with your swinging hand. Count "one" as you swing your left hand from shoulder height behind you down to the bottom of its arc at your side. Count "two" as you swing your left hand from the bottom of its arc at your side up to shoulder height in front of you. Count "three" as you swing your left hand from shoulder height in front of you back down to the bottom of its arc at your side. And finally, count "four" as you swing your left hand from the bottom of its arc at your side back up to shoulder height behind you.

STEP FIVE: As you continue to swing your hand, feel the centrifugal force pulling it "outward" along its arc, keeping your arm taut like the weight on the end of a string in a simple pendulum. Feel also a pulling or stretching sensation along your left side, just below the back of your left armpit, as your hand reaches the farthest point of its arc in front of you. Be sure not to bend your left arm as your hand reaches the farthest points along its arc.

If you are performing this drill correctly, the four counts will be of equal duration. Also, it will take you the same amount of time to go through the four counts on the 2 to 3 foot arc as on the shoulder height to shoulder height arc.

This preliminary drill helps to prepare you to find your golf swing tempo by teaching you the tempo and the rhythm of a simple pendulum that you can create with your body. This pendulum is similar to but slightly different than the golf swing pendulum. This drill also helps you to begin to feel the swinging motion of your left hand and the turning motion of your left shoulder. (See Illustration 2-1)

Address   ①   ②

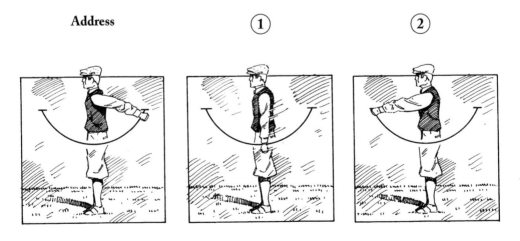

Illustration 2-1

Finding Your Golf Swing Tempo

Once you can comfortably perform the preliminary drill, you will be ready to find your golf swing tempo. The following drill will help you to find it:

STEP ONE: Stand erect, with the outsides of your feet as wide as the outsides of your shoulders, your hands hanging naturally at your sides, and your eyes looking straight ahead at the horizon. Make sure that there is no tension in either your shoulders, or upper arms.

STEP TWO: Curl each hand into a fist, again making sure that there is no tension in either your shoulders, upper arms or forearms. If you squeeze your upper arms and forearms with your opposite hand, they should feel "soft" and relaxed, not "hard" and tense.

STEP THREE: Tilt your upper body forward at the hips while flexing your knees slightly, so that you hang your arms and hands naturally in front of your body over a line formed by the toe of each shoe. If you are hanging your arms and hands correctly, you will feel a slight pulling or stretching sensation across the back of your shoulders, from the weight of your hanging arms and

Preliminary Drill

hands. Also, your hands will be turned in slightly, so that when you look down, the outer edge of each hand points in the direction of its respective hip, and you can see two knuckles on each hand.

STEP FOUR: Position your right arm at your side.

STEP FIVE: Keeping your feet in place, begin swinging your left hand to the right and back to the left in front of your body by turning your left shoulder to the right and back to the left. Begin by swinging your hand in 2 to 3 foot arcs, and then gradually extend the length of the arc until your left hand reaches at least shoulder height at the farthest points along its arc.

As you swing your left hand from the bottom of its arc up to shoulder height to your right, be sure to complete your shoulder turn to the right so that your left shoulder reaches a position underneath your chin when your left hand reaches the farthest point along its arc.

STEP SIX: As you continue swinging your left hand to the right and left in front of your body, count to four in time with your swinging hand. Count "one" as you swing your left hand from shoulder height to your left down to the bottom of its arc in front of you. Count "two" as you swing your left hand from the bottom of its arc in front of

Address   ①   ②

Illustration 2-2

you up to shoulder height to your right. Count "three" as you swing your left hand from shoulder height to your right back down to the bottom of its arc. Count "four" as you swing your left hand from the bottom of its arc back up to shoulder height to your left.

STEP SEVEN: As you continue to swing your left hand, feel the centrifugal force pulling it "outward" along its arc, keeping your left arm taut like the weight on the end of a string in a simple pendulum. Feel also a pulling or stretching sensation along your left side, from the back of your left armpit down to the outside of your left hip. Be sure not to bend your left arm as your hand reaches the farthest points along its arc.

If you are performing this drill correctly, the four counts will be of equal duration. Also, it will take you the same amount of time to go through the four counts on the 2 to 3 foot arc as on the shoulder height to shoulder height arc.

The time it takes you to count from 1 to 4 as you swing your left hand from the left to the right and from the right back to the left in front of your body is your optimum golf swing tempo. It's that simple. From now on, use your golf swing tempo with every club and on every swing. (See Illustration 2-2)

③ ④

Finding Your
Golf Swing Tempo

LEARNING AIDS

To help you to find and keep your golf swing tempo, I recommend that you use two learning aids.

Holding a 1 to 2 pound dumb bell or hand weight in your hand as you perform the drills outlined above will make it easier for you to feel the swinging motion in your hand, without adversely affecting the tempo of your swing. Remember, the amount of the weight at the end of the string does not affect the period of the simple pendulum, nor the tempo of the golf swing pendulum.

You can purchase dumb bells or hand weights at most sporting goods stores for less than $20. I recommend that you try the Heavyhands hand weights sold by SLM, Inc., P.O. Box 1070, Gloversville, NY 12078. You can call them toll free at (800)442-7440 to find a retail outlet near you.

Once you have determined your golf swing tempo, swinging your left hand in time to a metronome will also provide you with several benefits. First, it will keep you from rushing or dragging your golf swing tempo as you swing your left hand back and forth. Also, a metronome will help to ensure that each of the swing's four beats are of equal duration. Finally, once you set the metronome to your golf swing tempo, you will be able to immediately recall your tempo at any time during your practice sessions by simply turning on the metronome. This will become especially important when you begin swinging your left hand like a pendulum with a golf club in Chapters 4 and 5.

You can purchase a small, hand-held electronic metronome at most music stores for about $30. The Seiko Model DM-10 is an excellent product in this price range.

SUMMARY

In this chapter, you have learned the principles behind your golf swing tempo, along with a practical step-by-step approach to finding it. This chapter also introduced you to two learning aids that will make it easier for you to find and keep your golf swing tempo.

In the next chapter, you will learn how to master the golf swing rhythm, which is the next step towards learning how to swing your hands like a pendulum during your golf swing.

How to Master The Golf Swing Rhythm

In this chapter, you will learn how to master the golf swing rhythm, which is the next step in the series of steps you must follow to learn how to swing your hands like a pendulum during your golf swing.

Understanding The Golf Swing Rhythm

Recall that the rhythm of the simple pendulum is the division of the pendulum's period into four equal beats or counts. The simple pendulum swings from its starting point through the bottom of its arc to the farthest point of its arc in two beats, and then back through the bottom of its arc to the starting point in two beats.

The golf swing rhythm refers to how the total time of the golf swing pendulum is apportioned among the various parts of the golf swing. The total time it takes to complete the swing is apportioned among three parts: from address to the top of the back swing, from the top of the back swing to impact, and from impact to the finish. We call the first part the back swing, the second part the down swing and the third part the follow-through.

To understand the golf swing rhythm, think of the back swing as a complete swing of the golf swing pendulum in one direction, and the downswing and follow-through as a complete swing of the golf swing pendulum in the opposite direction. If you treat the golf swing pendulum like a simple pendulum and divide it into four equal beats or counts, the back swing will take two beats, and the combined downswing and follow-through will take two beats. Count "one-two" during the back swing, "three" during the downswing to impact and "four" during the follow-through to the finish. This 2:1:1 ratio is the golf swing rhythm! (See Illustration 3-1)

Unlike the golf swing tempo, which varies from person to person, the golf swing rhythm is universal. It is the same for everyone! Like your golf swing tempo, however, the golf swing rhythm is the same for every club and for every swing.

Address   **①**   **②**

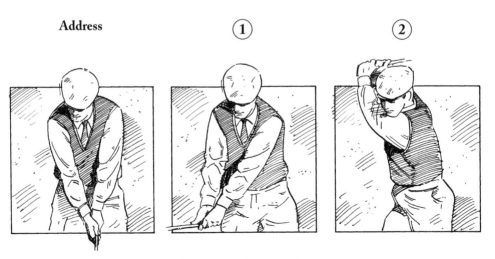

Illustration 3-1

MASTERING THE GOLF SWING RHYTHM

To master the golf swing rhythm, perform the following drill:

STEP ONE: Find your golf swing tempo by following the seven step drill in Chapter 2.

STEP TWO: Once you have found your golf swing tempo, stop swinging your left hand and allow it to hang naturally at the bottom of its arc in front of you.

STEP THREE: Count "one-two" to yourself at your golf swing tempo as you swing your left hand 2 to 3 feet to the right. Then count "three" to yourself at your golf swing tempo as you swing your hand to the left, back to the bottom of its arc, and "four" as you swing it 2 to 3 feet past the bottom of its arc to the farthest point of its fol-low-through. (See Illustration 3-2)

Understanding the
Golf Swing Rhythm

Repeat Step Three several times until you can perform
the drill smoothly at your golf swing tempo.

STEP FOUR: Once you can perform Step Three
smoothly at your golf swing tempo, stop swinging your
left hand and again allow it to hang naturally at the bottom of its arc in front of you.

STEP FIVE: Count "one-two" to yourself at your golf
swing tempo as you swing your left hand to the right
until it reaches shoulder height. Then count "three" to
yourself at your golf swing tempo as you swing your hand
to the left, back to the bottom of its arc, and "four" as you
swing it past the bottom of its arc back to shoulder height
on the follow-through.

As you swing your left hand from the bottom of its arc up
to shoulder height to the right, be sure to complete your
shoulder turn to the right so that your left shoulder
reaches a position underneath your chin when your left

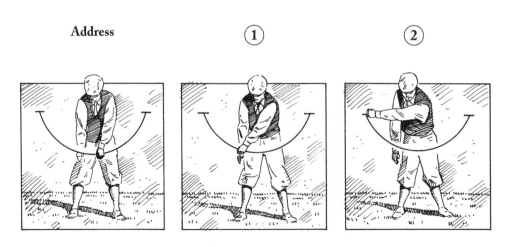

Address   ①   ②

Illustration 3-2

hand reaches the farthest point along its arc. If you are turning your left shoulder correctly, you will feel a pulling or stretching along your left side, from the back of your left armpit down to the outside of your left hip. (See Illustration 3-3)

Repeat Step Five several times until you can perform the drill smoothly at your golf swing tempo.

If you are performing this drill correctly, the four counts of the swing will be of equal duration. This means that the two counts of the back swing will be of the same duration as the two counts of the combined downswing and follow-through. Also, it will take you the same amount of time to go through the four counts on the 2 to 3 foot arc as the four counts on the shoulder height to shoulder height arc.

③　　　④

Mastering the
Golf Swing Rhythm

LEARNING AIDS

To help you to master the golf swing rhythm, I recommend that you use the same two learning aids introduced in Chapter 2. They will provide you with the same benefits while you are mastering the golf swing rhythm as they did while you were finding your golf swing tempo.

SUMMARY

In this chapter, you have learned the theory behind the golf swing rhythm, along with a practical step-by-step approach to mastering it for yourself. In the next chapter you will learn how to combine your golf swing tempo with the golf swing rhythm to swing your hands like a pendulum with every club.

Address   ①   ②

Illustration 3-3

③

④

Mastering The
Golf Swing Rhythm

CHAPTER FOUR

HOW TO SWING YOUR HANDS LIKE A PENDULUM WITH EVERY CLUB

In this chapter, you will learn how to combine your golf swing tempo with the golf swing rhythm to swing your hands like a pendulum during a full swing with every club. First though, you must establish a stable foundation for your golf swing pendulum by learning how to hold the golf club properly and how to properly position yourself and the golf club to the golf ball. In golf parlance, holding the club and positioning yourself to the ball are referred to as the address fundamentals and include grip, stance, posture, aim, hand position and ball position.

UNDERSTANDING THE ADDRESS FUNDAMENTALS

This chapter will not present a lengthy explanation of the address fundamentals. Many of golf's most famous players and teachers have already done an excellent job of explaining these fundamentals in the large number of books on golf instruction available on the market today. I encourage you to take advantage of one or more of these books by adding them to your golf library.

Because of the quality of instruction and the authors' places in history, I personally recommend Bobby Jones' *Bobby Jones On Golf*, Tommy Armour's *How To Play Your Best Golf All The Time*, Ben Hogan's classic *Five Lessons: The Modern Fundamentals of Golf*, and Jack Nicklaus' *Golf My Way*. Of course there are numerous other books that will help you in this area. These books are simply my favorites.

This chapter will instead present only those particular aspects of the address fundamentals that are essential to your ability to swing your hands like a pendulum during your golf swing. With this foundation in place, this chapter will then provide you with a step-by-step method of teaching you how to swing your hands like a pendulum during your full golf swing.

Grip — Because the grip is your only contact with the golf club, I believe it is the most important address fundamental. As you have learned earlier in this book, your hands swing back and forth in front of your body when you are swinging your hands like a pendulum. As a result, it is important that you hold the golf club so that you can move your hands easily in either direction. You will be able to move your hands most easily in either direction if you place your hands on the golf club in a way that is similar to the way in which your hands hang naturally at your sides or in front of your body.

To understand this aspect of the grip, go back to Step Three of the second drill in Chapter 2. From this position, bring your hands together in front of you, with the right hand below the left as if you are holding a golf club. If you are doing this correctly, you will still be able to look down and see two knuckles on each hand.

It doesn't really matter whether you use an overlapping or interlocking grip to hold the club. There are plenty of great players who have used each method. Personally, I prefer a grip with the little finger of my right hand overlapping the index finger of my left hand. Regardless of which method you choose, however, it is critical that you place your hands on the club in their "naturally hanging" manner.

In his all-time best selling *Little Red Book*, the late Harvey Penick suggests that you hold the golf club like it's a fine musical instrument. I can't agree more with his suggestion. I believe his suggestion refers to how your fingers curl around and make contact with the golf club.

Next time you are watching a band or orchestra perform, notice how the flutists, clarinetists, saxophonists and trumpet players curl their hands around their instruments. Or, next time you are watching your favorite rock, country or jazz band, notice how the guitarists hold their guitars. Pay particular attention to how the fingertip pads of each finger, including the thumb, makes contact with the instrument. In a correct golf grip, your fingertip pads will make contact with the golf club in a very similar fashion.

You can use an ordinary golf towel to help you to get this sense for how your fingers twine around the golf club. Begin by holding one end of the rolled-up towel loosely in your left hand, as if it were the grip of one of your golf clubs. With your right hand, grab the towel about 3" to 4" away from your left hand and tug slightly, resisting the tug with your left hand.

Notice how the fingers of your left hand coil around the towel in response to the tug of your right hand. Notice also how the fingertip pads of all five fingers of your left hand are the primary contact points with the towel. Switch the positions of your hands on the towel to get the same sense with the fingers of your right hand.

Finally, in order to swing your hands like a pendulum during your golf swing, it is very important that you hold the club with a relaxed grip pressure or with what some have referred to as "soft" hands. If you hold the club too tightly, you will create tension in your forearms, upper arms and shoulders, which will destroy the swinging motion of your hands. Of course, if you hold the club too loosely, you will lose control of the golf club.

To find your correct grip pressure, squeeze and relax your hands several times in succession as you hold the golf club. The "relaxed" grip pressure that results from this exercise will allow you to swing your hands like a pendulum during your golf swing.

Stance — Just as your grip is your only contact with the golf club, your stance is your only contact with the golf course. Your stance provides the foundation that supports your golf swing pendulum.

When you swing your hands like a pendulum, your hands will swing the same distance during the backswing as they will during the follow-through. Your stance must allow this to happen by allowing your upper body to turn equally in each direction. A "square" stance — one in which lines formed across your feet, knees, and hips are all parallel to the target line — is the only stance that will allow your upper body to turn equally in each direction.

If your stance is correct, your weight will be distributed evenly across both feet. Your weight will also be distributed evenly between the balls of your feet and the heels of your feet, and between the insides of your feet and the outsides of your feet. The balance you create in the address position is then maintained during the swing by the centrifugal force created by the swinging motion of your hands.

One way to check your balance is to curl your toes up in your shoes as you address the ball. If your weight is distributed correctly, curling your toes up will not affect your balance.

Posture — Your posture refers to the amount of flex necessary in your knees and hips to tilt your upper body forward to place the clubhead behind the golf ball. You must tilt your upper body far enough forward to place the clubhead behind the ball and to allow your hands to swing freely in front of your body, but not so far forward that you lose your balance or inhibit your ability to turn your shoulders.

To swing your hands like a pendulum during your golf swing, your hands and arms must extend naturally from your shoulders, with no tension in either your shoulders or your arms. You must never reach excessively for the ball with your hands and arms. If your shoulders and arms are relaxed, you will feel a slight pulling or stretching sensation across the back of your shoulders, from the weight of your extended arms, hands and golf club.

You must also keep your chin up so that your left shoulder can turn underneath it during the backswing, and your right shoulder can swing underneath it during the follow-through.

To find your correct posture, stand erect with your eyes looking at the horizon. After taking your grip and stance, extend the club directly out in front of you, with the hands and clubhead at approximately waist height, and the clubshaft parallel to the ground. Next, without changing the angle of the wrists, lower your arms until the clubhead is about knee high in front of you. From this position, bend at the hips until the clubhead touches the ground. Finally, flex the knees slightly to create good balance. Do not reach for the ball. Do not lower your chin.

One way to further stabilize the foundation of the golf swing pendulum is to feel as though you are slightly bowed out at the knees at address. This feeling is similar to the feeling you might have if you were sitting on top of a horse. If your knees are bowed correctly, you will feel a pulling or stretching across the inside of both thighs. Maintaining this tension in your inner thighs at the start of your swing will help you to turn rather than sway during the backswing.

Aim — Your aim is determined primarily by the direction
of the plane created by your golf swing pendulum. Recall
that in a simple pendulum, the weight and string always
swing back and forth in the same vertical plane. The
direction of the plane is defined by the swinging string,
which runs between the suspension point and the weight.

The plane of your golf swing pendulum is defined by
your swinging left arm. The angle of the plane is determined by the tilt of your upper body. The direction of
the plane is determined by the direction of the line
formed by your shoulders.

In order to start the flight of the ball directly at the target, you must address the ball so that the line formed by
your shoulders is parallel to the target line. If your shoulders are open, the plane will be pointed left of the target
and the ball will start on a line left of the target.
Conversely, if your shoulders are closed, the plane will be
pointed to the right of the target and the ball will start on
a line to the right of the target.

Whether the ball remains on its initial line of flight
depends upon the direction of the clubface. In order to
keep the ball on its initial line of flight, you must align
the clubface at a 90 degree angle to the line of your
shoulders. If you align the clubface at an angle of more
than 90 degrees to the line of your shoulders, the ball will
fade or slice from its initial line of flight. If you align the
clubface at an angle of less than 90 degrees to the line of
your shoulders, the ball will draw or hook from its initial
line of flight.

Hand Position— Hand position, or the position of your hands in relation to the axis of your golf swing pendulum, is the second most important address fundamental after the grip.

In the golf swing pendulum, your hands reach their fastest speed at their equilibrium point, which is the point directly below the suspension point or top of the spine. You must position your hands so that when viewed from the front the intersection of your left and right hand is even with your spine when your shoulders are parallel with the target line. The intersection of your left and right hand is the point where the crease in the heel of your right hand contacts the side of your left thumb. If you position your hands in relation to your spine in this way, and then swing your hands like a pendulum, you will always strike the ball at the precise moment that your hands and the clubhead achieve their maximum speed. Positioning your body in this way will also ensure that the initial flight of the ball will be directly at the target.

A quick way to check that your hand position is correct make sure that at address the intersection of your left and right hand is in line with your belt buckle or the zipper on your pants.

The **Address Position**

Illustration 4-1

Ball Position — Ball Position, or more correctly the position of your body in relation to the ball, is easy to determine once you have established the correct grip, stance, posture and hand position. Your ball position is correct if you have a correct grip, stance, posture and the clubface is square to the ball. If the clubface appears open, it is likely that you have positioned the ball too far back in your stance. If the clubface is closed, you have probably positioned the ball too far forward in your stance. To adjust the ball position, simply rotate your hands to the right or left, while maintaining the correct hand position, and then adjust your stance accordingly. You will find that the ball is correctly positioned ahead of your hand position with the woods and longer irons, and even with or slightly behind your hand position with the middle and shorter irons.

The address position shown in Illustration 4-1 incorporates all of the address fundamentals described above.

UNDERSTANDING THE FULL GOLF SWING

At this point, you have already learned most of what you need to understand the full golf swing. You have learned that you must swing your hands like a pendulum during your golf swing, and that you must use the same tempo and rhythm with every club and on every shot. You have also learned how to hold the golf club properly and how to properly position your body and the golf club to the golf ball.

Before we go on, it is essential that you understand that the basic motion of the full golf swing is the same for every club. After all, your grip is the same, your hand position is the same and your aim is the same. All that changes from club to club is the width of your stance, the tilt of your upper body, your distance from the ball and the length of your swing arc. And even these adjustments are relatively minor.

For example, to maintain your balance, you must take a slightly wider stance with the longer clubs than with the shorter clubs. To allow your arms to extend naturally and still reach the ball, you must tilt your upper body forward more and stand closer to the ball with the shorter clubs. When you tilt your upper body forward more with the shorter clubs, you naturally restrict your upper body's ability to turn, which results in a shorter swing arc with the shorter clubs than with the longer clubs.

It is also essential that you understand the important role that your upper back and shoulders play in the golf swing. In the golf swing pendulum, you support the weight of your extended arms, hands and club with your upper back and shoulders. You control the length of the swing arc and the speed of your hands through the turning motion of your shoulders, especially your left shoulder. To make a full swing, you must complete your shoulder turn to the right so that your left shoulder reaches a position underneath your chin when your hands reach their farthest point along their arc. In fact, you may find it helpful to think of a full swing as a "full turn".

Finally, you must understand that to gain greater distance in the full swing you simply choose a longer club. You do not change your swing. No matter which club you choose, you must still swing your hands like a pendulum and maintain your golf swing tempo and the golf swing rhythm.

Address

① ②

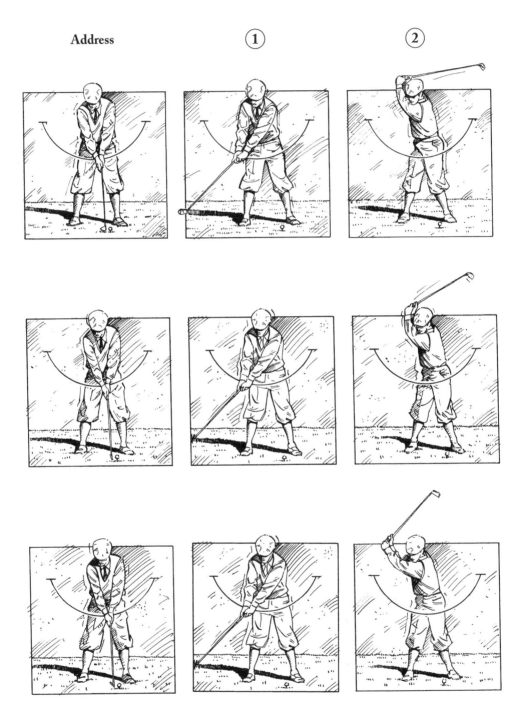

Illustration 4-2

Full Swing
with **Driver**

Full Swing
with **6-Iron**

Full Swing
with **Wedge**

Many golfers mistakenly believe that you must swing faster or harder with the longer clubs, especially the driver. It is true that your hands are moving faster at impact with the longer clubs because they are traveling along a longer swing arc. The clubhead is also moving faster with the longer clubs because of the combined effect of the faster hand speed and the longer clubshaft. These are the natural results of swinging your hands like a pendulum during the golf swing, however, and require no extra speed or power from you.

In fact, the longer the club, the more important it is that you maintain your golf swing tempo and the golf swing rhythm. The longer clubs are already more unwieldy and difficult to control than the shorter clubs. Trying to swing them faster or harder makes them even more difficult to control.

For instance, think of trying to hit a nail with a hammer that has a 16" handle as compared to a hammer with a 6" handle. If you consciously try to swing faster or harder with the longer hammer, it becomes more difficult to hit the nail, not easier. The same holds true with the full golf swing.

Illustration 4-2 demonstrates how the basic motion of the full golf swing is the same for every club.

PREPARING FOR THE FULL GOLF SWING

The following drill will help you to prepare for the full golf swing. This drill is similar to the drill you performed to find your golf swing tempo in Chapter Two, except that you will now use a golf club instead of a 1 to 2 pound dumb bell or hand weight. I recommend that you

begin with a pitching wedge and then gradually increase
the length of the club you use as you become more proficient with this drill:

STEP ONE: Stand erect, with the outsides of your feet
as wide as the outsides of your shoulders, your hands
hanging naturally at your sides, and your eyes looking
straight ahead at the horizon. Make sure that there is no
tension in either your shoulders, or upper arms.

STEP TWO: With your left arm still hanging naturally
at your side, take your grip with your left hand. As you
take your grip, make sure that there is no tension in either
your shoulders, your left upper arm or your left forearm.
It is important that you hold the golf club with a relaxed
grip pressure.

STEP THREE: Tilt your upper body forward at the
hips while flexing your knees slightly, so that you extend
your arms and hands naturally in front of your body over
a line formed by the toe of each shoe. Make sure that the
clubface is square to an imaginary target line and that you
can see two knuckles on your left hand.

If you are extending your arms and hands correctly, you
will feel a slight pulling or stretching sensation across the
back of your shoulders, from the weight of your extended
arms and hands. You will feel a slightly greater pulling or
stretching across the back of your left shoulder, because of
the added weight of the golf club in your left hand.

STEP FOUR: Let your right arm hang at your side.

STEP FIVE: Keeping your feet in place, begin swinging your left hand to the right and back to the left in front of your body by turning your left shoulder to the right and back to the left. Begin by swinging your hand in 2 to 3 foot arcs, and then gradually extend the length of the arc until your left hand reaches at least shoulder height at the farthest points along its arc.

As you swing your left hand from the bottom of its arc up to shoulder height to your right, be sure to complete your shoulder turn to the right so that your left shoulder reaches a position underneath your chin when your left hand reaches the farthest point along its arc.

STEP SIX: As you continue swinging your left hand to the right and left in front of your body, count to four in time with your swinging hand. Count "one" as you swing your left hand from shoulder height to your left down to the bottom of its arc in front of you. Count "two" as you swing your left hand from the bottom of its arc in front of you up to shoulder height to your right. Count "three" as you swing your left hand from shoulder height to your right back down to the bottom of its arc in front of you.

Illustration 4-3

Count "four" as you swing your left hand from the bottom of its arc in front of you back up to shoulder height to your left.

STEP SEVEN: As you continue to swing your left hand, feel the centrifugal force pulling it "outward" along its arc, keeping your left arm taut like the weight on the end of a string in a simple pendulum. Feel also a pulling or stretching sensation across the back of your left shoulder as it completes its turn to the right.

Make sure that you do not bend your left arm as your hand reaches the farthest points along its arc. Also make sure that you do not consciously manipulate the clubhead with the fingers of your left hand. Instead, allow the clubhead to respond naturally to the centrifugal force created by the pendulum swing of the left hand. (See Illustration 4-3)

As you become more proficient with this drill, your tempo with a golf club will be the same as your tempo with the dumb bell or hand weight. Your tempo will also be the

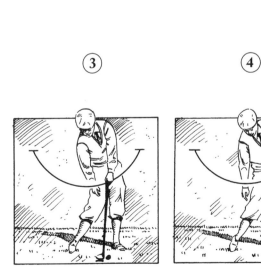

Preparing For The
Full Golf Swing

same with the longer clubs as with the shorter clubs. Keep repeating this drill until you can swing a club back and forth with your left hand as many as 40 or 50 times in a row. To avoid injury, begin with a lower number of repetitions and gradually work up to 40 to 50 repetitions.

MASTERING THE FULL GOLF SWING

In this section, you will combine your address fundamentals with your golf swing tempo and the golf swing rhythm to master the full golf swing. As in the previous section, I recommend that you begin with a pitching wedge and then gradually increase the length of the club you are using as you begin to master the full golf swing with the shorter clubs. I also recommend that you place your practice ball on a low tee. By placing the ball on a tee, you can focus your attention on swinging your hands like a pendulum during the full golf swing and not worry so much about striking the ball.

STEP ONE: After placing your practice ball on a low tee, find your golf swing tempo by following the seven step drill in Chapter 2.

Address   **①**   **②**

Illustration 4-4

STEP TWO: Once you have your golf swing tempo in
mind, stand 2 to 3 yards directly behind the golf ball and
pick out your target and target line. Also, visualize the
line parallel to the target line where you plan to place
your feet.

STEP THREE: From your position behind the ball,
take your grip, making sure that you can see two knuckles
on each hand with the clubface square to the line of your
shoulders.

STEP FOUR: With the club in your hands, approach
the ball from behind and to the left. As you get closer to
the ball, step forward with your right foot, tilt your upper
body forward and allow your arms, hands and golf club to
extend naturally from the back of your shoulders.
Suspend the clubhead behind the ball, just off the
ground, making sure that the clubface is at a 90-degree
angle to the target line.

STEP FIVE: Swing your left foot forward and place it
on a line parallel to your target line.

STEP SIX: Step to the right with your right foot and
place it on the same line as your left foot. Make sure that

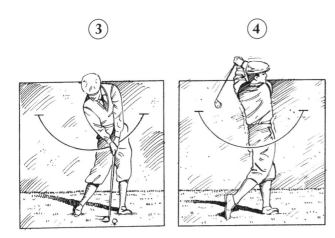

Mastering The
Full Golf Swing

your knees, hips and shoulders are also parallel to the target line. Bow your knees out slightly to stabilize the foundation of your golf swing pendulum. Check to see that the intersection of your left and right hand is aligned with your spine and the clubface is square to the target line.

STEP SEVEN: Begin the backswing by turning your shoulders to the right. Count "one-two" to yourself at your golf swing tempo as you swing your hands up and back to the top of the backswing. Then count "three" to yourself at your golf swing tempo as you swing your hands back to the bottom of their arc, and "four" as you swing through the follow-through and up and around to the finish. If your ball position is correct, you will hit the ball on the count of "three", although it is better to think of swinging through the ball on "three" on your way to the finish on "four".

As you swing your hands from the address position to the top of the backswing, make sure to complete your shoulder turn to the right so that your left shoulder reaches a position underneath your chin as your hands reach their position at the top of the backswing. You will feel a pulling or stretching sensation across the back of your left shoulder as it completes its turn to the right. Make sure that you do not bend your left arm as your hands reach the top of the backswing position.

Throughout the swing, feel centrifugal force pulling your hands outward along their arc. Do not consciously manipulate the clubhead with your hands. Instead, allow the clubhead to respond naturally to the centrifugal force created by the pendulum swing of your hands.

Illustration 4-4 demonstrates the full golf swing with a driver.

Summary

In this chapter, you learned how to combine the address fundamentals with your golf swing tempo and the golf swing rhythm to swing your hands like a pendulum during a full swing with every club. You learned that the basic motion of the full golf swing is the same for every club, with only minor adjustments in the width of your stance, the tilt of your upper body, your distance from the ball and the length of your swing arc. In the next chapter, you will learn to swing your hands like a pendulum with every swing.

How To Swing Your Hands Like A Pendulum With Every Swing

In this chapter, you will learn how to swing your hands like a pendulum with every swing. As used in this book, the phrase "every swing" refers to partial swings with particular clubs, especially the so-called scoring clubs. The scoring clubs have traditionally included the pitching wedge, the sand wedge and the putter. In more recent years, the concept of scoring clubs has been expanded to include "middle" wedges between the pitching wedge and the sand wedge, highly lofted "lob" wedges, and utility woods such as the seven-wood and nine-wood which are designed to take the place of the harder-to-hit long irons.

UNDERSTANDING THE PARTIAL GOLF SWING

You can produce a partial swing in one of three ways. You can shorten the length of the swing arc while using the full length of a club, you can make a full swing while "choking down" on the grip of a particular club, or you can combine both. Keep in mind that "choking down" on a club while making a full swing will not only shorten the length of the club, but it will have the added effect of shortening the length of your swing arc. Recall from Chapter Four that when you tilt your upper body forward to accommodate a shorter club, you naturally restrict your upper body's ability to turn, which results in a shorter swing arc with the shortened club.

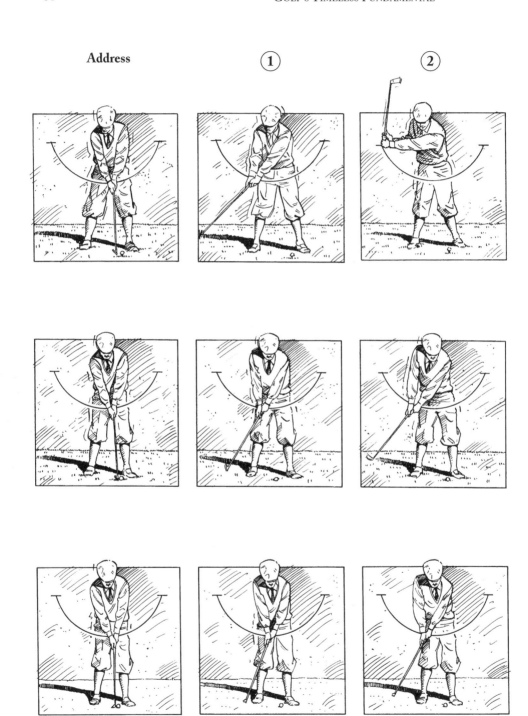

Illustration 5-1

③

④

Partial Swing
with **Wedge (Pitch)**

Partial Swing
with **Wedge (Chip)**

Partial Swing
with **Putter**

To swing your hands like a pendulum with every swing, you must understand that the motion for a partial swing is identical to the motion for a full swing. The only thing that changes is either the range of motion or the length of the club. You still support the weight of your extended arms, hands and club with your upper back and shoulders. You still control the length of the swing arc and the speed of your hands through the turning motion of your left shoulder. Finally, and probably most importantly, you still maintain your golf swing tempo and the golf swing rhythm. This is true during a partial swing with every club, including the putter. (See Illustration 5-1)

FEEL AND TOUCH DEFINED

Before teaching you how to swing your hands like a pendulum with each of the scoring clubs, I'd like to take a moment to define the terms feel and touch. Like tempo, rhythm and timing, these terms are routinely misunderstood and misused by most golfers. For most non-golfers, using the terms interchangeably will not create confusion. For golfers, the terms take on two distinct and very separate meanings.

The term feel describes our physical perception of the world around us. It involves nerve impulses that run from our skin and muscles to our brain. Feel is about physical sensations.

For example, you feel the texture of the grip against the skin of your fingers. You feel the weight of the club hanging in your fingers and fingertips. You also feel the weight of your extended arms, hands, and club across the back of your shoulders. Most importantly, you feel the pull of centrifugal force as you swing your hands like a pendulum during your golf swing.

Touch has less to do with physical sensations and more to do with knowledge of what to do in certain situations. Touch is the ability to know the type of shot called for, and how far to fly or roll the ball with that shot. Touch is heavily influenced by experience gained from past situations and your ability to imagine or visualize the required shot in new situations.

Much of what you need to know to dramatically improve your touch is easily learned. In fact, when you swing your hands like a pendulum during your golf swing, touch boils down to little more than knowing which club to use and how long a swing arc to use with that club. The following sections will provide you with practical guidelines about which club to use and the length of swing to use in certain commonly encountered situations.

Improving Your Pitching Touch

The pitch shot, as distinguished from the chip shot, is generally defined as a shot into a green that carries in the air farther than it rolls on the ground. A pitch shot might include a full swing with a pitching wedge from 120 yards out, or a partial swing with a lob wedge from as little as 10 yards out. Because the pitch shot can potentially cover such a wide range of distances, and because it accounts for a relatively large number of strokes during an average golfer's round, improving your pitching touch is crucial to your effort to lower your score.

The first step towards improving your pitching touch is to make sure that you have the right clubs. I recommend that your set of clubs contain the traditional 48-degree pitching wedge and 56-degree sand wedge, along with a 52-degree middle wedge and a 60-degree lob wedge.

Adding a middle wedge fills a "hole" that has traditionally existed between the pitching wedge and the sand
wedge. Adding a lob wedge allows you to make a full
swing on approach shots that might otherwise require
you to make a partial swing with one of your other
wedges. A lob wedge is also useful for shots from around
the green that you must fly high and land "soft".

The next step towards improving your pitching touch is
knowing which club to use. As suggested earlier, you can
decrease the distance you hit each of your wedges by
"choking down" on the grip. Typically, for every inch and
a half that you choke down on the grip with a full swing,
you will decrease the distance of the club by 8 to 10 yards.
A standard grip is long enough to allow most golfers to
comfortably choke down by as much as three inches.
This means that each wedge actually contains three separate wedges that cover a range of distance of between 16
and 20 yards. When deciding which club to use, you can
effectively choose from one of 12 wedges!

The final step towards improving your pitching touch is
to know how long a swing to use. If you take advantage
of all "12" wedges, you can cover the distance from 120
yards out to 25 yards out with just 2 swings — a full
swing from 120 yards down to 50 yards, and a partial

swing from 60 yards down to 25 yards. The following table presents the range of distances you can cover while making a full swing with each of your 12 wedges:

Wedge	Full Length	1.5" Choke	3" Choke
48-degree	120 yards	110 yards	100 yards
52-degree	105 yards	95 yards	85 yards
56-degree	85 yards	75 yards	65 yards
60-degree	70 yards	60 yards	50 yards

Of course, the maximum distance that you will hit each of your wedges may vary from the distances contained in this table. As a result, I recommend that you determine for yourself the maximum distance that you hit each of your wedges with a full swing and create a similar table that matches your game.

For pitch shots of less than 60 yards, I recommend that you use one partial swing with each of your 12 wedges. To determine the length of the partial swing that you will use on pitch shots from inside of 60 yards, determine the swing length necessary to hit your 48-degree wedge approximately 60 yards, including roll. For most golfers, this will not be any more than a one-half swing. Then, use that same length of swing with your middle wedge, sand wedge and lob wedge and determine the distance you hit the ball with each club. Once you have these distances, you can create a table for pitch shots of less than 60 yards, similar to the one that you created for your full swing wedges.

When you are making a partial swing, it is very important that you concentrate on swinging your hands like a pendulum by maintaining your golf swing tempo and the golf swing rhythm. If you are swinging your hands correctly, your follow-through will be the same length as your back swing.

Also, keep in mind that the ball spins less with a partial swing than with a full swing. As a result, the ball will tend to fly lower and roll more with a partial swing with a particular club than with a full swing with that same club. This is something you will need to take into account when you are calculating distances for your table.

IMPROVING YOUR TOUCH FROM THE SAND

The green side sand shot is simply a pitch shot with a few adjustments in your address position to take into account the texture of sand compared to turf. Unlike the pitch shot, however, you do not have to decide which club to use. The sand wedge is the only club that you will use from a green side bunker.

With the sand shot, you must grip the sand wedge with a very open club face. Then, as you address the ball, suspend the club head approximately two ball widths behind the ball with the leading edge of the club face square to the target line. Finally, take your stance with your feet, knees, hips and shoulders all parallel to each other, but open to the target line. As you take your stance, make sure that your arms, hands and club extend naturally from the back of your shoulders, with the intersection of your hands aligned with your spine.

If you have addressed the ball correctly, it will appear as though the ball is positioned forward in your stance, just opposite your left heel. In fact, the ball position only appears to be forward as a result of the open club face and stance. In reality, your hands are aligned with your spine when viewed from a 90-degree angle to your shoulders and therefor your swing plane.

To execute the sand shot, swing your hands like a pendulum, striking the sand with the club head two ball widths behind the ball. As your hands move through the bottom of their arc, centrifugal force will slide the clubhead through the sand under the ball. Unlike a pitch shot from the turf, the clubhead never strikes the ball during a sand shot. Instead, the clubhead strikes the sand, which in turn carries the ball out of the sand bunker.

To improve your touch from the sand, you must remember that a swing with a sand wedge from the sand will produce a shot that carries about one-half as far as a swing of the same length from the turf. This is because the clubhead slows down as it slides through the sand. Consequently, if you normally hit your sand wedge 85 yards with a full swing from the turf, your maximum distance with a full swing from the sand will only be 40 to 45 yards. On partial swings, you can adjust accordingly.

IMPROVING YOUR CHIPPING TOUCH

The chip shot is any shot from around the green that rolls on the ground farther than it carries in the air. A chip shot might include a pitching wedge from 2 or 3 yards off the edge of the green to a pin 3 or 4 yards on the green. It might also include a 3-iron from 2 or 3 yards off the front of the green to a pin in the back, 25 to 30 yards from the ball. Unlike the pitch shot, which can call for either a full swing or a partial swing, the chip shot always calls for a partial swing.

The first step towards improving your chipping touch is to select the right club. When chipping, always select the club with the least amount of loft necessary to carry the rough or fairway between the ball and the green. Your goal is to get the ball on the green and rolling as quickly as possible.

This approach has two benefits. First, it is easier to judge the distance that a ball will roll after carrying a short distance than it is to judge the distance that a ball will roll after carrying a long distance. Second, the margin of error for a miss hit with a shorter swing is greater than the margin of error for a longer swing.

The following method will help you to determine which club to select for a chip shot. First, pick out a spot on the green, 1 to 2 yards from the edge, on a line between the ball and the hole. The distance from the ball to this spot is the distance that the ball must carry. The distance from this spot to the hole is the distance the ball must roll. You can measure both of these distances by pacing them off.

Next, determine the ratio of carry to roll by dividing the distance the ball must carry to the target spot by the distance the ball must roll to the hole. For example, if you must carry the ball 2 yards and roll the ball 2 yards, your carry/roll ratio is 2:2 or 1:1. If you must carry the ball 2 yards and roll the ball 10 yards, your carry/roll ratio is 2:10 or 1:5. (See Illustration 5-2) Once you have your carry/roll ratio, use the following table to select the correct club:

Carry/Roll Ratio	Club
1:1	Sand Wedge
1:2	Pitching Wedge
1:3	9-Iron
1:4	8-Iron
1:5	7-Iron
1:6	6-Iron
1:7	5-Iron
1:8	4-Iron
1:9	3-Iron

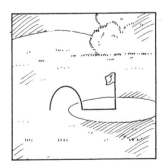 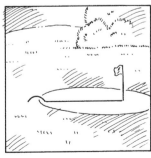

Carry/Roll Ratio
of 1:1 and 1:5

Illustration 5-2

This table is simply meant to provide you with guidelines for club selection. You may decide to select a more lofted club or less lofted club to take into account actual playing conditions that will affect the distance the ball will roll. For example, if the table suggests a 7-iron, but the chip shot is down hill, you may decide to select an 8-iron or even a 9-iron, instead.

Finally, as you address the ball, choke down on the grip about an inch and a half, and open your stance slightly. Choking down will provide you with better distance control, while an open stance will make it easier for you to swing your hands in front of your body on the follow-through.

Your swing need only be long enough to carry the ball to the target spot on the green with the loft of club you have selected. The ball will then roll the remaining distance to the hole. As you swing, avoid succumbing to the impulse to "hit" or "pop" the ball by manipulating the clubhead with your hands.

You will find that most chip shots call for a relatively short swing. In fact, it is unlikely that you will ever need to use more than a one-quarter swing during a chip shot. If you find it necessary to use more than a one-quarter swing, you may want to reconsider the club you have selected.

Improving Your Putting Touch

Because you do not have to worry about club selection, the key to improving your putting touch is consistently rolling the ball the correct distance. Of course, you must also read the green correctly and pick out the correct line. More "three putts" come from an inability to gauge the correct distance, however, than come from an inability to read the correct break.

Swinging your hands like a pendulum during your putting stroke is the best way to consistently roll the ball the correct distance. When you swing your hands like a pendulum, you do not have to think about how hard to "hit" the putt. Instead, you only have to think about the length of the swing while maintaining your golf swing tempo and the golf swing rhythm. In other words, you only have to think about swinging your hands like a pendulum with the correct swing length.

The popularity of long putters in recent years underscores the importance of a pendulum swing during the putting stroke. In fact, a long putter is nothing more than a simple pendulum. With the long putter, the suspension point is your left hand as it holds the butt of the club against your sternum. The shaft is the string and the clubhead is the weight. You control the length of the swing and the speed of the clubhead with your right hand and arm. The chief advantage of the long putter is that you only have to think about swinging the clubhead like a pendulum with the correct swing length.

Once you learn to swing your hands like a pendulum during your putting stroke, you will never need to resort to the long putter. Your putting stroke will already possess all of its advantages. All you will need to learn is a method for finding the correct swing length for a putt of a particular distance. Before teaching you that method, it is necessary to review a few address fundamentals for putting.

Your address fundamentals for the putt are very similar to your address fundamentals for the full swing, with a few adjustments. I recommend that you putt with a reverse overlap grip, in which the index finger of your left hand overlaps the little finger of your right hand. This will help your left hand to lead the way during the putting stroke. Also, it is important that you adjust your posture so that both of your eyes are positioned directly over the target line. To swing your hands like a pendulum during your putting stroke, your arms, hands and club still must extend naturally from the back of your shoulders, with the intersection of your hands aligned with your spine.

To learn how to find the correct swing length for the putt, go to a level spot on a practice green and place several balls 10 feet from a hole. Next, find your golf swing tempo by following the seven step drill in Chapter 2. Putt several balls at the hole, being sure to maintain your golf swing tempo and the golf swing rhythm. Concentrate on making a smooth, rhythmic pendulum swing. As with the chip shot, avoid succumbing to the impulse to "hit" or "pop" the ball by manipulating the clubhead with your hands. Keep putting until you have found the correct swing length to consistently roll the ball 10 feet.

Estimate how many inches the putter head swings back from the ball on your 10 foot putt. Divide the length of the swing by 10 feet to calculate a ratio of inches of swing per foot of roll. For example, if you swing the putter head back 10 inches on a 10 foot putt, your swing/roll ratio is 1 inch per foot.

Once you know your swing/roll ratio, you simply multiply the length of any level putt by your swing/roll ratio to find the length of swing necessary to roll the ball that distance. Thus, if your swing/roll ratio is 1 inch per foot, you will need to swing the putter head back 18 inches if you are faced with an 18-foot putt. This method of determining swing length is fairly accurate for putts of up to 25 feet.

Of course, you will need to adjust your swing/roll ratio for uphill or downhill putts. You will also need to adjust your swing/roll ratio from course to course. I recommend that you "re-calibrate" your swing/roll ratio on the practice green before each round. While this method is not fool-proof, and is no substitute for the kind of experience that only comes with time, it will provide you with a practical guideline from which you can immediately improve your putting touch.

SUMMARY

In this chapter, you learned how to swing your hands like a pendulum during partial swings with the scoring clubs. You also learned that when you swing your hands like a pendulum, choosing the right club and swing length are the keys to improving your touch. This chapter then offered you practical guidelines for choosing the right club and swing length in certain commonly encountered situations. In the next chapter you will learn how to apply these guidelines to swing your hands like a pendulum on the golf course.

How To Swing Your Hands Like A Pendulum On The Golf Course

In this chapter, you will learn how to swing your hands like a pendulum on the golf course. You will learn this during a simulated "playing lesson" that begins with your arrival at the golf course, and ends with several holes of golf. In this playing lesson, you will have an opportunity to apply the guidelines that you learned in the previous chapter, along with the knowledge you have accumulated throughout the first four chapters of this book.

This lesson will take place on one of my favorite courses in Colorado. After you have completed this lesson, I recommend that you repeat the lesson on a course with which you are familiar. In fact, an excellent way to practice is to play your home course, or other courses that you play frequently, from time to time in your mind's eye.

Arriving At The Golf Course

You arrive at the course about an hour before your scheduled tee time. After checking in and purchasing a small bucket of range balls, you head to the practice green to hit a few putts. By beginning on the practice green, you give yourself a chance to warm up slowly, focusing mainly on the "small" muscles of your hands and forearms.

Find a level spot on the practice green and place several
range balls 10 feet from the hole. Next, find your golf
swing tempo by following the seven step drill in Chapter
2. To help you feel the swing, I recommend that you
hold one or two range balls in your left hand as you perform the drill.

Go back to this drill often during your round. It provides
your golf swing with the same benefits that a conductor
provides to a band or orchestra. The conductor sets and
maintains the tempo during the performance of a musical
piece. Without the conductor, the musicians can get out
of synch with each other, and may rush or drag under the
pressure of performance. Without this drill, the different
parts of your body may get out of synch with each other,
and you may rush or drag your golf swing.

Putt several balls at the hole, being sure to swing your
hands like a pendulum at your golf swing tempo and the
golf swing rhythm. As you putt the first few balls, concentrate on making a smooth, rhythmic swing. Then,
before you finish putting, "re-calibrate" your swing/roll
ratio for the day's round.

Once you are finished putting, head over to the chipping
and pitching green to hit a few chip shots. Place several
balls far enough from your target spot on the green to
create a carry/roll ratio to the cup of 1:5. Again, find
your golf swing tempo by following the seven step drill in
Chapter 2.

Using your 7-iron, chip several balls to the target spot,
allowing the balls to roll the remaining distance to the
cup. Be sure to swing your hands like a pendulum at your
golf swing tempo and with the golf swing rhythm. Avoid
succumbing to the impulse to "hit" or "pop" your chip
shots by manipulating the clubhead with your hands.

From the chipping and pitching green, it's time to move
to the practice range. I recommend that you start with a
few partial swings with one of your wedges before
increasing your range of motion to a full swing. During
your full swing warm-up, hit two or three balls with every
second or third club.

For example, after making two or three full swings with
your wedge, make two or three full swings with your 8-
iron, your 6-iron, your 4-iron and so on. Complete your
full swing warm-up by hitting two or three swings with
your driver. To paraphrase the great Ben Hogan, if you
hit more than 15 balls before your round, you aren't
warming up, you're practicing.

Throughout your warm-up, concentrate on swinging your
hands like a pendulum. If you are having a difficult time
maintaining your golf swing tempo and the golf swing
rhythm, go back to your address fundamentals in Chapter
4, and then repeat the tempo and rhythm drills in
Chapters 2 and 3.

Whatever else you do, avoid experimenting with "quick
fixes" or "tips" from other golfers on the range. You
already know everything you need to know to consistently
hit the ball long and straight. If you have confidence in
your knowledge and ability, you will begin to see consistent progress toward your goals.

STEPPING TO THE FIRST TEE

Just as you finish warming up, the starter calls your group to the first tee. The first hole is a 362-yard dogleg left par 4, slightly downhill from the tee to the landing area in the fairway. Trees line the entire left side of the hole, with a fairway bunker on the inside of the dogleg, approximately 240 yards from the tee. A 10 to 15 mile per hour wind is blowing right to left out of the west.

Because the length of the hole does not require that you hit your driver, you select your 3-wood to take the fairway bunker out of play. After teeing your ball on the left side of the tee box, you pick out a target line down the right center of the fairway. Next, you find your golf swing tempo, first without your club in your hands and then while making a couple of practice swings with your club. With your golf swing tempo clearly in mind, you take your grip and address the ball. From this point forward, you concentrate only on swinging your hands like a pendulum.

To swing your hands like a pendulum, you begin your backswing with your left shoulder. You count "one-two" to yourself at your golf swing tempo as you swing your hands to the top of your backswing. Then "three-four" to yourself at your golf swing tempo as you swing your hands back through the bottom of their arc and the follow-through to the finish. On the count of "three" centrifugal force swings the clubhead into the back of the ball and you watch as the ball sails 230 yards down the center of the fairway.

Counting to yourself during your swing provides you with
several benefits. First, it helps you to concentrate on
making a smooth, rhythmic pendulum swing. Also, by
concentrating on a positive thought such as counting to
four at your golf swing tempo, you clear your mind of any
negative thoughts. Your mind cannot entertain a positive
thought and a negative thought at the same time.
Finally, by counting to yourself at your golf swing tempo,
you neutralize the "hit impulse" that destroys the tempo
and rhythm of most golf swings.

The yardage marker on the sprinkler head nearest to your
ball tells you that you have about 130 yards to the center of
the green. With the pin cut in the left front corner, however, you estimate that the shot will play more like 120
yards. Because of the severe slope of the green, you want
to make sure that you leave your next shot below the hole.

You select your pitching wedge, address the ball, and
make a full swing at your golf swing tempo. The ball
lands 8 feet from the cup and spins back another 2 feet,
leaving you a 10-foot putt straight up the hill.

Before the round you determined that your swing/roll
ratio for the greens on this course is 1":1'. This means
that ordinarily you would make a 10-inch backswing for
this 10-foot putt. Because it is uphill, you decide that it
will play more like a 12-foot putt and will therefor call for
a 12-inch backswing.

You make a couple of practice swings, concentrating only on your golf swing tempo, the golf swing rhythm and the correct swing length. You address the ball with your eyes directly over the target line, take one last look at the cup, and then swing your hands like a pendulum. As with every shot, you count "one-two" to yourself during the backswing and "three-four" during the downswing and follow-through up to the finish. This results in a smooth, rhythmic stroke that rolls the ball 10 feet up the hill and into the center of the cup. BIRDIE!

ON THE SECOND TEE

The second hole is a 429-yard par 4, slightly uphill from the landing area in the fairway to the green. With a steady 10 to 15 mile per hour wind in your face, and a high-faced bunker carved into the right side of the fairway some 220 yards from the tee, you know you will have your work cut out for you.

This time you select your driver and choose a target down the center of the fairway. While standing behind the ball, you remind yourself that your golf swing tempo and the golf swing rhythm is the same with your driver as it was with your pitching wedge on the last hole. All that changes is the length of your arc. This mental note will help you to maintain your tempo and rhythm under circumstances that might otherwise tempt you to "over swing".

You swing your hands like a pendulum and lace a 250-yard drive down the left side of the fairway, leaving you about 180 yards to the middle of the green. It seems that the wind had little effect on such a well-struck ball. The spring in your step as you walk up the fairway is a sure sign that your self-confidence is growing.

Assessing your next shot, you notice that the pin is cut in the back right corner of the green. The entrance to the green is flanked by large sand bunkers. You estimate that the location of the pin, the change in elevation and the head wind will combine to add a total of 20 yards to your next shot. You pull a 3-iron from your bag and complete your address procedure.

As you begin your backswing, fear plants a seed of self doubt into your mind. "Maybe it's a 2-iron instead of a 3-iron." In that instant, you speed up your tempo and pull the ball just short of the bunker left of the green. You realize that even if you had needed one more club, you would have been better off trusting your swing and maintaining your golf swing tempo and golf swing rhythm. Worst case, you might now be in the middle of the green instead of short and left.

Upon arriving at your ball, you immediately pace off the distance from your ball to a target spot about 2 yards onto the green. You also pace off the distance from the target spot to the cup. You determine that you have 4 yards from your ball to the target spot and 20 yards from the target spot up the sloping green to the cup. Ordinarily, a carry/roll ratio of 1:5 would call for a 7-iron. You select a 6-iron to make sure that you get the ball up the slope and back to the cup.

You take several practice swings at your golf swing tempo as you measure the length of swing necessary to carry the ball to the target spot. You focus only on the target spot, knowing that if you hit the target spot, the club you have chosen will roll the ball the remaining distance to the cup. This time you swing your hands like a pendulum while counting to yourself at your golf swing tempo, watching eagerly as the ball jumps off the clubface, lands just past the target spot and rolls 5 feet past the cup. Your par putt coming back lips out, you tap in for your bogey and head to the next tee having learned a good lesson.

ON THE THIRD TEE

The third hole is a 180-yard uphill par 3 with an elevated green that conceals most of the putting surface from your vantage point on the tee. Two bunkers guard the green front left and center, with a third bunker ready to catch shots that stray long and left. Today the pin is cut front and center, just over the lip of the bunker. The 10 to 15 mile per hour wind is now quartering into you from the right.

You select a 5-iron because the tee shot is uphill and into the wind. You take a moment to re-establish your golf swing tempo and move through your address procedure. Swinging your hands like a pendulum with good tempo and rhythm, you watch as the ball climbs towards the pin into a now stiffening wind. In the last few yards the wind takes some distance off the shot and the ball catches the top lip of the bunker. It rolls down the face and settles in the sand at the bottom of the bunker.

Walking off the tee, you realize that you can sometimes make a good swing and still end up in a bad place. Rather than getting down on yourself for ending up in the bunker, you recognize that you simply misjudged the effect of the wind on the ball. You now turn your attention to making the best of the shot at hand.

As you step into the bunker with your sand wedge, you remind yourself that a sand shot is simply a pitch shot with a few adjustments to account for the soft texture of the sand. You open the clubface, suspend the clubhead over the sand two ball widths behind the ball, square the leading edge of the clubface to the target line and settle into the sand with an open stance. You then swing your hands like a pendulum while counting to yourself at your golf swing tempo.

When you reach the count of "three" the clubhead strikes the sand two ball widths behind your ball. Centrifugal force slides the clubhead through the sand under the ball and a cushion of sand carries the ball onto the green. After two short hops, the ball spins to a stop 4 feet short of the cup. You sink your par putt and walk off the third green at even par for the round!

ON YOUR WAY

You continue to swing your hands like a pendulum during
the rest of your round, focusing on your golf swing tempo
and the golf swing rhythm. You have some good holes
and some bad holes, but realize that you are on your way
to playing golf at a consistently higher level than you ever
have before. You finish your round with a score that is 6
strokes lower than your previous low score for the year, on
what you now realize was a very challenging course. You
feel a renewed sense of self-confidence and can hardly
wait for your next round with your regular foursome.

CONCLUSION

Congratulations!

You have reached the conclusion of this book and are now ready to begin a journey towards your goal of playing the best golf of your life. You will soon be hitting the golf ball consistently longer and straighter than you ever have before. You will see a dramatic improvement in your short game. In a short time, you will be scoring lower and winning more. Your self-confidence will begin to rise and you will soon experience a new sense of respect and admiration from your golfing friends.

By completing this book, you have opened yourself to a whole new way of looking at the golf swing. You have discovered that swinging your hands like a pendulum during your golf swing is golf's timeless fundamental. You have also learned:

- how to find your golf swing tempo, which is the first step towards learning how to swing your hands like a pendulum during your golf swing;

- how to master the golf swing rhythm, which is the next step towards learning to swing your hands like a pendulum during your golf swing;

- that your golf swing tempo and the golf swing rhythm are the same for every club and for every swing;

- how to combine the address fundamentals with your golf swing tempo and the golf swing rhythm to swing your hands like a pendulum during a full swing with every club;

- that the basic motion of the full golf swing is the same for every club, with only minor adjustments in your width of stance, the tilt of your upper body, your distance from the ball and the length of your swing arc;

- how to swing your hands like a pendulum during partial swings with the scoring clubs;

- and finally, how to swing your hands like a pendulum on the golf course.

You have an opportunity to remove the mystery surrounding the golf swing once and for all. . . if you are willing to follow the step-by-step method presented in this book.

Even though you have reached the end of this book, I hope that our journey together is just beginning. I want to continue to be part of your success as you begin to achieve and surpass the goals you have set for yourself. I also want to be there to help you through any rough spots that you may encounter on your path to success.

I am especially interested in hearing from you about ways that I can improve this book and the method of learning golf that it contains. For instance, you may discover new insights about the golf swing that add to the insights presented in this book. You may also discover new golf products that will help others to learn the method offered here. By learning from you, I can continue to improve the quality of the golf instruction that I am providing to others.

So please stay in touch! I hope to hear from you soon.